Do Beavers Eat Poutine?

COOL CANADIAN QUIZZES

H. Becker

Scholastic Canada Ltd.

Toronto New York London Auckland Sydney
Mexico City New Delhi Hong Kong Buenos Aires

Scholastic Canada Ltd.
604 King Street West, Toronto, Ontario M5V 1E1, Canada

Scholastic Inc.
557 Broadway, New York, NY 10012, USA

Scholastic Australia Pty Limited
PO Box 579, Gosford, NSW 2250, Australia

Scholastic New Zealand Limited
Private Bag 94407, Botany, Manukau 2163, New Zealand

Scholastic Children's Books
Euston House, 24 Eversholt Street, London NW1 1DB, UK

www.scholastic.ca

Library and Archives Canada Cataloguing in Publication

Becker, Helaine, 1961-, author
Do beavers eat poutine? : cool Canadian quizzes / H. Becker.

ISBN 978-1-4431-5762-9 (softcover)

1. Canada--Miscellanea--Juvenile literature. I. Title.
FC58.B39 2017   j971   C2016-907987-2

For photo credits please see inside back cover.

6 5 4 3 2 1   Printed in Canada 139   17 18 19 20 21

MIX
Paper from
responsible sources
FSC® C103567

Table of Contents

What's Your Canadian Name?. 4

In Shape or Out of Shape?. 6

Which Way to Wawa?. 8

Do Beavers Eat Poutine?. 12

It's Official!. 14

Hockey Trivia Faceoff. 17

Canadian Star Power! 21

Would You Survive in the Arctic Wilderness? 24

What Province or Territory Are You? 33

How Canadian Are You? 37

Are You an All-Canadian Sports Fan? 39

Test Your Canadian History IQ 42

What in the World Is . . . ? 45

How Weird Is Canada? 47

The Maple Leaf Olympics 49

Are You Ready for Prime (Ministers) Time?. 53

Made in Canada 55

For Loons Only! 57

For Canuckleheads Only! 59

Canada Counts! 61

Whirl-a-Word 63

Canada's Best Spy Agent — You! 64

Extreme Canada. 66

Would You Survive as a Voyageur? 69

What Iconic Canadian Animal Are You?. 75

Are You Ship Shape? 78

Book a Trip to Canada! 81

What Extremely Delicious Canadian Food Are You?. 83

Could Albertosaurus Eat Your Homework? 85

Would You Triumph as a Backcountry Flying Ace? 88

O Canada! Eh?. 92

Laura Secord Saves the Day — or Does She? 93

What's Your Canadian Name?

Using the chart on the next page, find the initial of your first name, the initial of your last name and the number of your birthday to get your Canadian name. For example, if your name is **J**ohn **M**acdonald and your birthday is January **13**, then your Canadian name is Crazy Otter Gretzky Labradoodle.

First Name Initial		Last Name Initial		Birthday	
A	Moose	A	Poutine	1	Nehani
B	Big Bear	B	"The Snowflake"	2	Whitehorse
C	Wiarton Willie	C	Beavertail	3	Brantford
D	Icefisher	D	Sugarpie	4	of the Muskeg
E	Mad Squirrel	E	Snowshoe	5	Mayor of Banff-Guelph
F	Sir Walrus	F	Cod Tongue	6	Temagami
G	The Narwhal of	G	Ski-Doo	7	Kamloops
H	Beluga	H	Fiddle	8	Timmins
I	Porcupine	I	Zamboni	9	Norway House
J	Crazy Otter	J	"The Rocket"	10	of the Klondike
K	Weasel	K	Igloo	11	de Saguenay
L	Walleye	L	"Big Red"	12	Tundra Flower
M	Muskie	M	Gretzky	13	Labradoodle
N	Coho	N	Pine Cone	14	Yellowknife
O	Fierce Chipmunk	O	"Gee-Haw"	15	de Louisbourg
P	Lobster	P	Gold Nugget	16	Mississauga
Q	Grey Owl	Q	Maple Leaf	17	Moose Jaw
R	Eagle	R	Frozen Toe	18	Whistler
S	White Raven	S	Regina-Victoria	19	Gander
T	Loonie	T	Hab	20	From the Land of the Midnight Sun
U	Great Grizzly	U	Inuksuk	21	of the North Pole
V	Angry Elk	V	Hat Trick	22	de Nord
W	Snow Goose	W	Mukluk	23	Mount Royal
X	Spirit Bear	X	"The Honest Mountie"	24	From the Crowsnest Pass
Y	Blackfly	Y	Maple Syrup	25	Baffin
Z	Skeeter	Z	Cheese Curd	26	Canuck
				27	From Where the Snow Flies
				28	Horsefly
				29	Wawa
				30	Flin Flon
				31	True North

5

In Shape or Out of Shape?

How well do you know Canada's provinces and territories?
Match the shapes on the left to the correct names on the right.

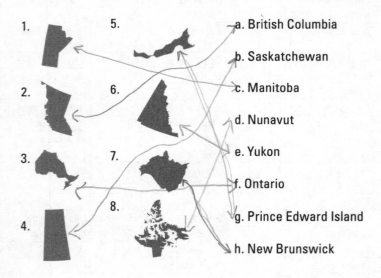

1.

5.

a. British Columbia

b. Saskatchewan

c. Manitoba

2.

6.

d. Nunavut

e. Yukon

3.

7.

f. Ontario

8.

g. Prince Edward Island

4.

h. New Brunswick

Bonus question: Which
provinces/territories are
NOT shown here?

Albreta
North West territories
Nova SLosia
Newfoundland and labrodor
(\$ + qubec)

SCORING

Give yourself one point for each correct answer to questions 1 to 8. Give yourself one additional point for each province or territory you correctly named for the bonus question.

1. c	5. g	Bonus question:
2. a	6. e	Newfoundland and
3. f	7. h	Labrador, Quebec, Northwest
4. b	8. d	Territories, Nova Scotia,
		Alberta

HOW YOU RATE . . .

0-2 Out of shape. Are you sure you live in Canada?

3-7 Shape-shifter. You're the party type — you like to mix it up!

8-12 Shaping up. Soon you will be a super★!

13 Shipshape. Your knowledge of Canada knows no bounds!

Which Way to Wawa?

Can you match these very real places to the Canadian province or territory you will find them in?

1. Vulcan
   a. Saskatchewan
   b. Northwest Territories
   c. Alberta
2. Flin Flon
   a. Manitoba
   b. Ontario
   c. New Brunswick
3. Punkeydoodle's Corners
   a. Ontario
   b. British Columbia
   c. Newfoundland and Labrador
4. Snowball
   a. Ontario
   b. Yukon
   c. Nunavut
5. Eyebrow
   a. Alberta
   b. British Columbia
   c. Saskatchewan
6. Cape Onion
   a. Nova Scotia
   b. Prince Edward Island
   c. Newfoundland and Labrador
7. Saint-Louis-du-Ha! Ha!
   a. New Brunswick
   b. Manitoba
   c. Quebec

8. Blubber Bay
   a. Quebec
   b. British Columbia
   c. Nova Scotia
9. Belcher Islands
   a. Nunavut
   b. Saskatchewan
   c. New Brunswick
10. Mermaid
    a. British Columbia
    b. Quebec
    c. Prince Edward Island
11. Nuttby
    a. Quebec
    b. Prince Edward Island
    c. Manitoba
12. Jerrys Nose
    a. Newfoundland and Labrador
    b. Alberta
    c. Northwest Territories
13. Mayo
    a. Nova Scotia
    b. Quebec
    c. Manitoba
14. Baldy Hughes
    a. Quebec
    b. Ontario
    c. British Columbia
15. Horsefly
    a. British Columbia
    b. Alberta
    c. Yukon

16. Mushaboom
    a. Manitoba
    b. Saskatchewan
    c. Nova Scotia
17. Crotch Lake
    a. Newfoundland and Labrador
    b. Northwest Territories
    c. Ontario
18. Poopoo Creek
    a. British Columbia
    b. Manitoba
    c. Yukon
19. Moose Factory
    a. Manitoba
    b. Saskatchewan
    c. Ontario
20. Moose Jaw
    a. Saskatchewan
    b. Manitoba
    c. Ontario

SCORING

Give yourself one point for each
correct answer.

1. c	11. a
2. a	12. a
3. a	13. b
4. a	14. c
5. c	15. a
6. c	16. c
7. c	17. c
8. b	18. a
9. a	19. c
10. c	20. a

HOW YOU RATE . . .

0-2 Place name newb. Don't worry, you can always move to Hope, British Columbia.

3-10 Place holder. You're getting somewhere. But that might be Nowhere Island, Ontario.

11-18 Second place. Almost there — but "there" might be Foxtrap, Newfoundland and Labrador.

19-20 Place ace. You've arrived at the winner's circle — in Toogood Arm, Newfoundland and Labrador!

Do Beavers Eat Poutine?

The beaver is one of Canada's best-known national symbols. How well do you know everyone's favourite furry mascot?

1. True or false: Beavers are the largest rodents on earth.
2. Beavers use their tails to slap the water in order to . . .
   a. warn intruders to stay away.
   b. warn other beavers of danger.
   c. both a and b.
3. The largest beaver dam in the world is in Wood Buffalo National Park, Alberta. It is visible from space! How long is it?
   a. 8,000 m
   b. 850 m
   c. 500 m
4. The scientific name for the type of beaver that lives in Canada is . . .
   a. Castor canadensis.
   b. Bevrus canadensis.
   c. Rodentor dentor.
5. True or false: A beaver's teeth continue to grow throughout its lifetime.
6. What products, made from beaver fur, were so popular in Europe that they contributed to Canada's exploration and settlement by Europeans?
   a. Fur coats.
   b. Felt hats.
   c. Hudson's Bay blankets.
7. In Haida legend and lore, the beaver represents . . .
   a. persistence and teamwork.
   b. the trickster.
   c. foolishness.

8. The beaver's home is called a . . .
   a. burrow.
   b. dam.
   c. lodge.
9. True or false: Beavers are vegetarians.
10. How many fingers do beavers have on each paw?
   a. Three.
   b. Four.
   c. Five.

SCORING

Give yourself one tail-slap point for each correct answer.

1. False. They're the second largest. Capybaras are the largest.

2. c	5. True	8. c
3. b	6. b	9. True
4. a	7. a	10. c

HOW YOU RATE . . .

0-3 Beaver beginner. It's fun to build beaver know-how!

4-7 Beaver B+. You have earned the right to smack your tail down hard!

8-10 Beaver best in class. You may even be part beaver. Check your teeth.

It's Official!

Can you brag with the best of them about how well you know
Canada? Test your knowledge with Canada's official symbols.

1. Which of these three pictures shows Canada's official coat of arms?

   a.   b.   c.

2. The maple tree is one of Canada's official symbols. Which of the
    tree silhouettes below is a maple tree?

   a   b.   c.

3. What is the official name of Canada's national anthem?
    a. "True North, Strong and Free."
    b. "O Canada."
    c. "Home and Native Land."

4. True or false: One of Canada's national symbols is the Canadian
    horse.

5. Canada has two official sports. What are they?
    a. Ice hockey and lacrosse.
    b. Ice hockey and curling.
    c. Lacrosse and ringette.

6. What are Canada's official colours?
   a. Red, white and blue.
   b. Red, green and yellow.
   c. Red and white.
7. What object from nature is shown on the Canadian flag?
   a. A pine cone.
   b. An oak leaf.
   c. A maple leaf.
8. Canada's national motto is *A Mari Usque Ad Mare*. It's in Latin. What does it mean in English?
   a. From Sea to Sea.
   b. The Iron Horse Rules the North.
   c. We Hold the Crown Close.
9. In what year did Canada get its current flag?
   a. 1867
   b. 1965
   c. 1685
10. Which of these symbols is an official symbol of Canada?
    a. The inuksuk.
    b. The beaver.
    c. The moose.
11. Canada's national bird is the . . .
    a. blue jay.
    b. grey jay.
    c. oh jay.
12. Canada's national bird has another name. It is the . . .
    a. whisky jack.
    b. apple jack.
    c. flap jack.

SCORING

Give yourself three points for each correct answer.

1. a	5. a	9. b
2. c	6. c	10. b
3. b	7. c	11. b
4. True	8. a	12. a

HOW YOU RATE . . .

0-9 Official beginner. Maybe you need more maple syrup in your diet!

12-24 Race official. Judging by your score, you're almost there!

27-36 Official winner. Don your red and white tuque and wear it with pride.

Hockey Trivia Faceoff

Are you a hockey hero or a hockey hopeful? Grab a friend and find out if you know these cold hard facts about Canada's favourite game.

1. True or false: The first Stanley Cup was made out of platinum.
2. What was the first year the Maple Leafs won the Stanley Cup?
   a. 1815
   b. 1915
   c. 1932
3. What was the last year the Maple Leafs won the Stanley Cup?
   a. 1917
   b. 1967
   c. 1987

4. Which team has won the most Stanley Cups?
   a. The Montreal Canadiens.
   b. The Toronto Maple Leafs.
   c. The Boston Bruins.
5. How many teams currently compete for the Stanley Cup?
   a. 25
   b. 30
   c. 31
6. What is Wayne Gretzky's nickname?
   a. The Hat Trickster.
   b. The Great One.
   c. Greatsky.
7. True or false: Girls have been active hockey players since the very beginnings of the game.

8. The "Original Six" are the NHL teams that played during hockey's "Golden Age," from 1942 to 1967. Name them. Maple, Canis

9. True or false: The Stanley Cup went for a ride on a roller coaster.

10. What were the first hockey pucks made out of?
   a. Rubber.
   b. Wood.
   c. Frozen horse or cow poo.

11. "Bucket" is slang for what important hockey item?
   a. The goal.
   b. The helmet.
   c. The Stanley Cup.

12. Which set of names includes one who was NOT a real hockey player?
   a. The Chicoutimi Cucumber, Jim "Cement Head" Hargreaves, Milt "Count of Sauerkraut" Schmidt.
   b. Gary "Suitcase" Smith, Max "Dipsy-Doodle-Dandy" Bentley, "Rocket" Richard.
   c. "Toe" Blake, "Ding Dong" McCrae, Bob "Battleship" Kelly.

13. What animal is sometimes thrown onto the rink by Red Wings fans?
   a. Birds.
   b. Octopuses.
   c. Snakes.

14. Which innovation had a huge impact on the game of hockey?
    a. Metal whistles were replaced with plastic ones, so whistles didn't freeze to referees' lips.
    b. Goalie pads were lined with lead to stop pucks from breaking players' legs.
    c. Everyone who attended a hockey game had to bring a hat for the famous "hat trick ceremony" that starts every match up.
15. How many Olympic gold medals have been won by Canada's men's hockey team? Give yourself an extra point if you know how many the Canadian women's team has won.
    a. 3
    b. 9
    c. 20

SCORING

Give yourself one point for each correct answer.

1. False
2. c
3. b
4. a
5. c
6. b
7. True. One of the first female players was Isobel Stanley, the daughter of the earl who gave the game its great prize, the Stanley Cup.
8. Give yourself one point for each team you got right: Montreal Canadiens, Toronto Maple Leafs, Boston Bruins, New York Rangers, Detroit Red Wings, Chicago Blackhawks.
9. True
10. c
11. b
12. c. The ringer is "Ding Dong" McCrae.
13. b
14. a
15. b. Give yourself an extra point if you knew the Canadian women's team has won 4.

HOW YOU RATE . . .

0-1 Rookie. Practise your slapshots — and brush up on your hockey history — to score big.

2-6 Left wing. You've left out a few winning answers, but you are still an asset to the team.

7-12 Right wing. You are on the right track to hockey trivia stardom.

13-18 Team captain. You've got a solid grip on your hockey stick, and on hockey trivia.

19-21 Leading scorer! You are the MVP of the Hockey Trivia League!

Canadian Star Power!

Some of the world's best-loved celebrities are Canadian from the tip of their tuques to the bottom of their hockey skates. How well do you know these Canadian standouts?

1. This Canadian superstar singer shares a name with a male duck. Who is it?
   a. John Gander.
   b. Drake.
   c. Donald Sutherland.

2. This Canadian astronaut brought a guitar to the International Space Station and conducted a singalong with thousands of kids back on Earth.
   a. Roberta Bondar.
   b. Tim Horton.
   c. Chris Hadfield.

3. This Canadian doctor discovered the treatment for the deadly disease diabetes.
   a. Sir Frederick Banting.
   b. Sir John Insule.
   c. Rose Fortune.

4. What did people call the reaction of fans to the music of Canadian singer Justin Bieber?
   a. Bieber Fever.
   b. Justin Time!
   c. Beep Beep.

5. This Canadian singer has sold more than 220 million albums worldwide and performed sold-out shows for years in Las Vegas, Nevada. Who is it?
   a. Michael Bublé.
   b. Céline Dion.
   c. Michael Jackson.

6. Which superstar comedian is NOT Canadian?
   a. Will Arnett.
   b. Mike Myers.
   c. Tina Fey.

7. This Hollywood pioneer was called "America's Sweetheart" as a star of silent films in the early years of the twentieth century. She was also a director, movie producer and one of the founders of United Artists. Who was she?
   a. Shirley Temple.
   b. Audrey Hepburn.
   c. Mary Pickford.

8. Canadian Measha Brueggergosman is celebrated worldwide for her incredible accomplishments as . . .
   a. an opera singer.
   b. an Olympic swimmer.
   c. a fashion designer.

9. What Canadian rock stars were once married to each other?
   a. Avril Lavigne and Chad Kroeger.
   b. Alanis Morissette and Gord Downie.
   c. Neil Young and Joni Mitchell.

10. Elijah McCoy is famous for an invention having to do with what?
    a. Refrigerators.
    b. Steam engines.
    c. The Canadarm for the International Space Station.
11. What famous Canadian inspired the nation and raised money for cancer research with his attempt to run across the country?
    a. Terry Fox.
    b. Rick Hansen.
    c. Lester Pearson.
12. Two of Hollywood's biggest box office draws are Canadian. And they share a first name. Who are they?
    a. Steve Martin and Steve McQueen.
    b. Brad Pitt and Brad Patt.
    c. Ryan Reynolds and Ryan Gosling.

SCORING

Give yourself one star for each correct answer.

1. b	4. a	7. c	10. b
2. c	5. b	8. a	11. a
3. a	6. c	9. a	12. c

HOW YOU RATE . . .

0-1 Celebrity so-so. You are less interested in the stars than in what's in your lunchbox.

2-5 Celebrate! Not for doing a stellar job on this quiz, but for something else that makes you happy. Go you!

6-8 Celebrity gawker. You are up on all things Superstar.

9-12 Canada's next celebrity! You've got star power, baby.

Would You Survive in the Arctic Wilderness?

You've thoroughly enjoyed your Arctic cruise through the Northwest Passage so far! You have seen polar bears and narwhals, siksiks and muskox. And you've met the most amazing people! You've especially enjoyed the pre-arranged day trips that take you off your posh ship and out onto the land.

1. Today, there are two options on the ship's bulletin board. You choose to . . .

   a. snap photos of a migrating caribou herd. > Go to question 2.

   b. learn how to identify Arctic plants and build an inuksuk. > Go to question 3.

2. Your guide makes sure you are warmly dressed and puts some extra gear you will need in a backpack. You . . .

   a. sling it over your shoulder. > Go to question 4.

   b. put it behind you in the dogsled. > Go to question 5.

3. You are deeply involved with examining the petals of a tiny tundra flower when you smell a terrible stink. You . . .

   a. look to your left. You see Marty, the other kid on the cruise ship. > Go to question 29.

   b. look to your right. You see a sasquatch and a polar bear. > Go to question 30.

4. You start walking. The scenery is stark — white sky, white snow. Your guide is in front of you, walking briskly. You try to keep up, but your shoelace comes undone. You bend to retie it, and when you get back to your feet, the guide is gone! You . . .

a. call out, "Hey! Guide! Where'd you go? > Go to question 6.
b. run in the direction you last saw her. > Go to question 7.

5. You've never been in a dogsled before. It's incredible — the silence all around, only the sound of the dogs' paws and their breathing. You are completely enchanted! You . . .
a. ask the guide if you can have a turn driving. > Go to question 25.
b. ask the guide what it takes to become a dogsled expert, like she is. > Go to question 26.

6. You feel a hand on your shoulder and you scream in shock. The guide laughs. "You have to pay more attention when you're out on the land. I circled behind you and you never even heard me. That's dangerous!" You . . .
a. bristle. That was totally uncool of her to sneak up on you like that and scare you. You say, "I'm outta here!" turn on your heel and head back to camp. > Go to question 8.
b. laugh. You say, "You really had me going there! I'll pay more attention from now on." You continue heading west. > Go to question 9.

7. You run and you run. You realize you are hopelessly lost. You . . .
a. open your emergency backpack. You take out your compass and figure out where you are, and how to get to the bay where the cruise ship is docked. Then you chart a course back to the ship, using landmarks to help you stay on track. > Go to question 19.
b. keep running. Eventually you stumble upon an inuksuk. You know it can tell you something about where to find sites on the featureless Arctic landscape. You decide to figure out what this inuksuk can tell you. > Go to question 20.

8. You stomp off toward camp. You walk about half a kilometre and start to cool down, maybe because the wind has picked up. You . . .
a. turn up your collar, shove your hands deeper into your pockets and start jogging as a way to warm up. > Go to question 16.
b. reach for your backpack to get out your extra windbreaker. > Go to question 17.

9. You walk farther out onto the land. It is very cold, but very beautiful. Your guide points at a herd of caribou in the distance. She signals you to get down on your belly and creep toward them.
a. You do exactly as she says. > Go to question 10.
b. You say, "That's so cool!" > Go to question 11.

10. To your utter surprise, your guide turns and runs, leaving you all alone. And then you realize why — the caribou are stampeding toward you! You . . .
a. take an ice pick out of your backpack and very quickly dig a ditch in the permafrost and slip into it. > The caribou run right over you — but you are unharmed! You make it back to the ship in one piece. ARCTIC SURVIVOR!
b. panic and run. Alas, caribou run faster. And they are coming right behind you! > Go to question 15.

11. Your guide whispers in your ear everything she knows about caribou behaviour. You come within photo-snapping distance. You are very excited, but very nervous. You put your camera to your eye. At just that moment, you notice something moving out of the corner of your eye. It's a polar bear! You . . .

a. freeze! > Go to question 12.

b. think, but remain calm and alert. > Go to question 13.

c. jump to your feet. Screaming loudly and flailing your arms wildly, you run straight for the polar bear. > Go to question 14.

12. The polar bear decides you look like a tasty dinner. > ARCTIC OOPS.

13. The guide glances up and sees the polar bear too. Your guide quickly shoots an emergency flare up in the air. It startles the bear, who dives into some open water and swims away. The caribou scatter and run away. You have not managed to get any photos, but you arrive back at the cruise ship with quite a story to tell. > ARCTIC SURVIVOR.

14. The polar bear takes one look at you and gets up on its hind feet and roars. You keep running for it. You get within a hair's breadth of the beast — so close you can smell its seal-stink breath. But just as you are about to rub noses, it turns and lopes away. It dives into the water and is gone! > ARCTIC SURVIVOR.

15. The thundering herd is gaining on you. You are almost out of hope. You put on one last push of speed and . . .

a. swerve left. > Whew! The caribou swerved right. You've escaped by a hair. ARCTIC SURVIVOR.

b. swerve right. > Oops. The caribou swerved too. You are now part of the permafrost. ARCTIC OOPS.

16. After a few more minutes of jogging, you're a lot warmer, but you realize that you should have reached the camp by now and it's nowhere in sight. You've been travelling in the wrong direction! You've made a grave mistake by separating from your guide. You . . .

    a. look at the sky and note the position of the sun. It is to your left, and it was to your right when you set out. You decide to keep walking in the direction you are going. You know camp — and the cruise ship — have to be straight ahead! Don't they? > Go to question 18.

    b. remember you have a very loud whistle in your coat pocket. You pull it out and blow. > A minute later, a caribou comes running straight at you and flattens you. ARCTIC OOPS.

17. Oh no! Your backpack's not there! You realize you had put your backpack down when you tied your shoelace, and left it on the ground. You are alone, and a storm is brewing. You have no supplies. You decide to . . .

    a. continue on your way back to camp. It must be close. > Go to question 33.

    b. go back and collect your backpack. > Unfortunately, you never find it, and the storm closes in, coating you in ice so thick you resemble a giant icy sasquatch. You stand there, immobile, for months, neither living nor dead. Then, a miracle happens! Hunters spot you! They manage to unthaw you, but you never return to normal. You can only peep like a tiny sad bird. An Arctic ptarmigan, perhaps. ARCTIC OOPS.

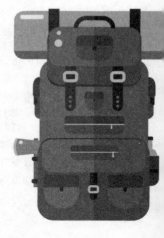

18. You keep walking and walking and walking. The next thing you know, you have arrived at a settlement. > ARCTIC SURVIVOR.

19. You walk for a while. You become cold and quite thirsty. You're so tired! How much farther can it be? You . . .

    a. check your compass again. > Go to question 21.

    b. check your watch. > Go to question 22.

20. As you study the inuksuk, you notice that the arms are perfectly aligned with the sun. You know the sun was low in the sky, and that you were walking toward it as you began your journey. Does the other arm then point to the harbour where the ship is docked? You also notice footprints all around the inuksuk. You . . .

    a. head in the direction that the inuksuk points. > You find yourself back at the harbour, but the ship is gone. ARCTIC OOPS.

    b. decide to wait for the owners of those footprints to come back. Someone will find you if you sit tight. > You are right. Before long, a band of very friendly walruses pull themselves out of the water and direct you back to the ship. ARCTIC SURVIVOR!

21. You discover the compass is broken! You've been going the wrong direction! You are in a quandary. How will you find your way with a broken compass? You . . .

    a. find a caribou bone, and stick it upright in the snow to make a compass using the sun and shadows as your guide. > Go to question 23.

    b. recognize the slight rise of land to your left. You believe the ship is in a bay just on the other side of it. You head for the hill and climb it. > Go to question 24.

22. You have been walking for an hour and you realize you are feeling the beginning signs of hypothermia. You know if your body temperature falls too low, you will get sleepy and freeze to death! You decide to . . .

a. hunker down to conserve energy. > Go to question 34.

b. drink the bottle of water in your backpack. > Go to question 35.

23. Your compass is a brilliant success. Using it, you can find your way back to the ship and safety. > ARCTIC SURVIVOR.

24. On the other side of the hill, exactly where you expected to find the ship, you find — nothing. Just more tundra. You cry. Your tears freeze all around your body and you become a pitiful Popsicle. > ARCTIC OOPS.

25. She says, "Sure! Let me teach you the commands." She hands you the reins. You . . .

a. shout,"Mush!" > Go to question 27.

b. say, "Wait a sec. I'm not ready!" > Go to question 28.

26. The guide looks at you and laughs. "Expert? I'm no expert! I'm one of the passengers on the cruise ship! I thought this would be fun to try, so I tied up the real guide in the ship's linen closet and pretended I was her. You and I are in for some REAL adventure!" You . . .

a. push the phony guide off the sled and take over. > You call out, "WHOA!" and bring the dog team to a stop. You light a flare and wait until the real guide comes with backup to collect you. You make it back to the ship in one piece, and with lots of doggy friends. ARCTIC SURVIVOR.

b. decide that sounds like fun! > You shout, "GEE!" and "HAW!" The dogs, following your commands, turn left, then right, then wind up running in circles until their harnesses are hopelessly tangled. The dogs bark and snap at you and your phony guide. You begin to think you made a serious mistake. You were right. ARCTIC OOPS.

27. The dogs take off. The guide was not quite ready, though. Uh-oh! She fell out of the sled — along with your backpack! And the dogs are running like crazy, leaving guide and gear in your icy dust. You

had paid very careful attention to the guide's instructions, so you know exactly what to do. You shout, "WHOA!" then "HEE," and "HEE" again so you are facing in the opposite direction. You shout, "MUSH!" but this time hold the reins a little more firmly. The dogs carry you and the sled back to your waiting guide, who hands you your backpack and gives you a pat on the back. You make it back to the ship in one piece. > ARCTIC SURVIVOR.

28. You weren't ready because your arm was caught in the strap of your backpack. The sled hits a rough patch. You can't control it! The sled goes flying up into the air. Somehow you have managed to turn the dogsled into a magical flying sled! You turn the sled left and right, admiring the stark, beautiful scenery. Then you feel the sled stall. And you feel yourself dropping like a stone. Down, down, down into the freezing cold Arctic Ocean. The last words you say are, "I told you so." > ARCTIC OOPS.

29. Marty has a very bad habit of wandering off, so you keep your eyes on him at all times. That's an excellent plan, except that you didn't realize you, Marty and your guide were being stalked by a pack of Arctic wolves. And they've already picked off the guide. So while Marty picked his nose, the wolves picked you. > ARCTIC OOPS.

30. You look at your guide. Your guide looks at you. You say . . .
    a. "Run!" > Go to question 31.
    b. "Wow! I didn't know sasquatches were real!" > Go to question 32.

31. The polar bear runs after you. The sasquatch runs after the guide. You would hate to see your guide eaten, so you . . .
    a. close your eyes. > The polar bear gets you. The sasquatch gets your guide. ARCTIC OOPS.
    b. reach for your backpack, pull out the emergency flare and throw it over your shoulder. > It bursts into flames behind you, melting a hole in the ice. The polar bear and sasquatch fall into the hole, giving you and your guide just enough time to make it back to camp safely. ARCTIC SURVIVOR.

32. "Of course we are," says the sasquatch. "It's polar bears that are make-believe!" At that, the polar bear fizzles away in a puff of snowflakes, leaving you to contemplate the sasquatch as it picks its teeth with something resembling a human leg bone. You realize, of course, that you must be dreaming. So you pick up some snow, make it into a seriously hard-packed snowball and throw it at the sasquatch. It hits bang between the beast's eyes. With a sad expression, the sasquatch fizzles away in a puff of snowflakes, and you wake up in your bed, with unusually cold toes. > ARCTIC SURVIVOR.

33. Lucky for you, camp was about twelve seconds away. You get a serious scolding from your mother, from the guide and from the cruise ship company, which immediately requires you to leave the ship forever — and there will be no refund. > ARCTIC SURVIVOR.

34. Hunkering down is a good idea, as long as you are in a warm, sheltered spot. But you are out on the Arctic tundra, fully exposed to the elements! Bad call. You are now a Popsicle. > ARCTIC OOPS.

35. Drinking water was a good idea. It gave you just enough energy to keep walking until you made it to camp and safety. > ARCTIC SURVIVOR.

What Province or Territory Are You?

Everyone has a secret "inner landscape." Which province or territory is a match for yours?

1. You prefer . . .
   a. basketball. > Go to question 2.
   b. soccer. > Go to question 3.
   c. reading. > Go to question 4.
   d. skiing. > Go to question 5.
2. Your favourite fruit is . . .
   a. peaches. > Go to question 6.
   b. pineapple. > Go to question 7.
   c. blueberries. > Go to question 8.
3. Which is your favourite Canadian coin?
   a. The loonie. > You are MANITOBA.
   b. The toonie. > You are SASKATCHEWAN.
   c. The nickel. > Go to question 4.
4. Which is your favourite school subject?
   a. Math. > Go to question 10.
   b. Science. > Go to question 11.
   c. Phys. ed. > You are ALBERTA.
   d. History. > You are QUEBEC.
5. You prefer . . .
   a. cats. > Go to question 8.
   b. dogs. > You are the YUKON.
   c. fish. > Go to question 12.
   d. hermit crabs. > You are NUNAVUT.
6. Which musical instrument do you prefer?
   a. The tuba. > You are ONTARIO.
   b. The woodwinds. > You are ALBERTA.
   c. That tinkly triangle thingy. > You are
   BRITISH COLUMBIA.

7. Which describes you best?
    a. Open-minded. > You are BRITISH COLUMBIA.
    b. Outgoing. > You are NEWFOUNDLAND AND LABRADOR.

8. Which kind of book would you prefer?
    a. Something funny. > You are NEWFOUNDLAND AND LABRADOR.
    b. Something that is full of weird facts. > You are NEW BRUNSWICK.
    c. A quiz book. > Go to question 9.
    d. A book about Anne of Green Gables. > You are PRINCE EDWARD ISLAND.
9. Do you usually root for the underdog or the reigning champion?
    a. Underdog. > You are ONTARIO.
    b. Champion. > You are QUEBEC.
    c. Neither. I root for the best team. > You are NOVA SCOTIA.
10. You prefer . . .
    a. board games. > You are MANITOBA.
    b. video games. > You are NEW BRUNSWICK.
11. Which would you rather be?
    a. A vet. > You are BRITISH COLUMBIA.
    b. An RCMP officer. > You are ONTARIO.
    c. A powerful politician. > You are QUEBEC.
12. Which do you prefer?
    a. Cooking. > You are the NORTHWEST TERRITORIES.
    b. Crafts. > You are NUNAVUT.
    c. Sports like rock climbing. > You are the YUKON.

YOU ARE...

Alberta. You are the strong, silent type. People look up to you.

British Columbia. If a tree falls in the forest, does it make a sound? You believe you know the answer, to this and to all other mysterious questions. You love polar fleece, orcas and dim sum.

Manitoba. You are very susceptible to flattery. You get along with everybody. Your favourite animals are prairie dogs because they are so, so cute.

New Brunswick. You sometimes experience extreme mood swings. You have a magnetic personality and high hopes, and you like chocolate so much you wish it flowed down the middle of your street in a lovely chocolatey brown river of deliciousness.

Newfoundland and Labrador. At times you seem to have a split personality. You have a great sense of humour but can also be standoffish. You love to open your mouth when you are eating and shout, "Seafood!"

Northwest Territories. You take a while to warm up to new people. You enjoy hanging out at home in your jammies. You can be very territorial.

Nova Scotia. You are musical and especially enjoy the soothing sound of a bagpipe band. You have a suspicious streak and try to fish for information from your friends. When you get cold, your nose turns blue.

Nunavut. You are very no-nonsense. You love all winter sports. You are the polar opposite of your best friend. Your favourite items of clothing are your giant fuzzy slippers.

Ontario. You are brash and bold. You love excitement and very tall things. You like doughnuts.

Prince Edward Island. You are exceptionally talented and even more humble. Your favourite colour is green. You secretly think your feet look like potatoes.

Quebec. You go your own way. You frequently worry that no one understands you. You have excellent taste, especially in woolly tuques and reindeer sweaters.

Saskatchewan. You can be a bit old fashioned, but you also have a strong independent streak. You like eating berries and singing at the top of your lungs, but not at the same time. Your favourite sport is skateboarding.

Yukon. You are not always as honest as you should be, but you have a heart of gold.

How Canadian Are You?

1. On a typical snowy day in February, your favourite activity is . . .
   a. drinking hot chocolate by the fire.
   b. playing shinny.
   c. a polar bear dip in the lake. Such frosty fun!

2. How many times a day do you typically say "I'm sorry"?
   a. 20 or more.
   b. 50 or more.
   c. Too many to count.

3. Which would you enjoy most?
   a. Carving a duck decoy.
   b. Training a Labrador retriever.
   c. Fishing for largemouth bass.

4. Which city would you most like to visit?
   a. Red Deer, Alberta. I like deer.
   b. St. John's, Newfoundland. I like lobster.
   c. Victoria, British Columbia. I like cities named for queens.

5. How much would you like to wear a "bunny hug"?
   a. A lot.
   b. Every day.
   c. I sleep in mine.
   d. What's a bunny hug?

6. If you wrote a song about Canada, you would call it . . .
   a. "Uh-Oh, Not Again. I Dropped My Homework in the Snowbank."
   b. "That Frosty Stuff on Your Scarf Is So cute, I Think I'm in Love."
   c. "Cold Feet, Warm Heart."

7. What does Canada mean to you?
   a. Milk in bags.
   b. "Land" or "settlement."
   c. Hockey on TV from August to July.

8. Your favourite colour is . . .
   a. Red, the colour of love.
   b. White, the colour of snow.
   c. Red and white, because they're Canadian.
9. Which do you say most?
   a. Eh?
   b. Aboot.
   c. Sorry.
10. What is the greatest number of mosquito bites you've ever had at one time?
   a. So many I was actually a giant mosquito bite.
   b. 5,000 or more.
   c. I never notice mosquitoes. It's the blackfly bites that really get me down.

SCORING

1. a3 b5 c7	3. a7 b5 c3	5. a7 b5 c3 d0	7. a7 b5 c5	9. a5 b2 c7
2. a3 b5 c7	4. a5 b5 c5	6. a5 b3 c7	8. a7 b7 c7	10. a5 b5 c10

HOW YOU RATE . . .

36 + You are 100% Canadian! Canadians come in every shape, every colour and every size. We are a delightfully quirky bunch, and extremely lucky to call this country home.

Are You an All-Canadian Sports Fan?

Sure, we love hockey — this is Canada, eh — but we also love lots of other Canadian sports. How well do you know these iconic Canadian pastimes?

1. Racing with dogs harnessed to sleds is called . . .
   a. mushing.
   b. mashing.
   c. smushing.
2. What sport uses these commands:
   Gee! = Right, Haw! = Left,
   Whoa! = Stop, and Hike! = Go.
   a. Horse racing.
   b. Dogsledding.
   c. Buffalo riding.

3. How long is the Yukon Quest, Canada's longest sled dog race?
   a. 1,609 km
   b. 161 km
   c. 42 km
4. What sport features a rock, a broom and a button?
   a. Squash.
   b. Ice fishing.
   c. Curling.

5. The town of West Pubnico, in Nova Scotia, got its name from a favourite Canadian sporting activity. It comes from a Mi'kmaq word meaning . . .
   a. a hole cut in the ice for fishing.
   b. long jump.
   c. paddle in a fast canoe.

6. What sport can be played in a "field" or a "box"?
   a. Badminton.
   b. Ringette.
   c. Lacrosse.

7. The game ringette is similar to hockey except . . .

   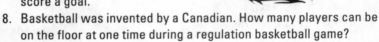

   a. it uses a straight stick.
   b. the goal is a bell-shaped hole in the ice.
   c. players ring a bell when they score a goal.

8. Basketball was invented by a Canadian. How many players can be on the floor at one time during a regulation basketball game?
   a. 10
   b. 5
   c. 7

9. What is the maximum weight of a curling stone?
   a. 18 kg
   b. 18.75 kg
   c. 19.96 kg

SCORING

Give yourself one maple-leaf-shaped gold medal for each correct answer.

1. a	4. c	7. a
2. b	5. a	8. a
3. a	6. c	9. c

HOW YOU RATE ...

0-2 Good sport! Thanks for taking the Canadian Sports Quiz!

3-5 Sports buff. Maybe you should spend more time doing your school work.

6-9 Sports star. Have you considered a career as a curling musher?

Test Your Canadian History IQ

How well do you know Canadian history?

1. Which explorer established the first French settlement in North America, in Quebec?
   a. Samuel de Champlain.
   b. Martin Frobisher.
   c. Sebastian Cabot.
2. Canada's first capital was . . .
   a. Toronto.
   b. Kingston.
   c. Halifax.
3. What year did Nunavut become an independent territory of Canada?
   a. 1948
   b. 1999
   c. 2012
4. Canada fought valiantly in World War I. Where in France is there a Canadian monument to our fallen soldiers?
   a. Vimy Ridge.
   b. Paris.
   c. Ypres.
5. An important battle took place on the Plains of Abraham in Quebec in 1759. It changed the course of Canadian history forever. What two countries fought this battle?
   a. Canada and the United States.
   b. Great Britain and France.
   c. Canada and Portugal.

6. Which people called the east coast of Canada "Vineland"?
   a. Vikings.
   b. Celts.
   c. Mi'kmaq.

7. In the 1890s, more than 100,000 people rushed into Canada's Yukon territory to try to find what valuable resource?
   a. Oil.
   b. Diamonds.
   c. Gold.

8. What year did Newfoundland join Confederation?
   a. 1949
   b. 1849
   c. 1749

9. In the fifteenth and sixteenth centuries, several European nations sent fishermen to Newfoundland every summer to harvest the plentiful stocks of cod they found there. They would add salt to the fish to preserve it and bring it home in vast quantities to feed their populations. What countries were they?
   a. England, Hungary, Norway and Sweden.
   b. England, France, Spain and Portugal.
   c. Spain, Portugal, Greece and Bulgaria.

10. A British poet named Henry Wadsworth Longfellow wrote a famous tragic poem about a French Canadian woman whose beloved dies in her arms. What is the poem called?
    a. "Hiawatha."
    b. "Evangeline."
    c. "Sainte-Marie among the Hurons."

11. The Canadian Pacific Railway helped make Canada a country by building a transcontinental rail line that linked central Canada to British Columbia. It was completed in 1885. What is this historic event called?

    a. The Great Rail Race.
    b. Connect the Dots.
    c. The Last Spike.

SCORING

Give yourself one point for each correct answer.

1. a	3. b	5. b	7. c	9. b	11. c
2. b	4. a	6. a	8. a	10. b	

HOW YOU RATE . . .

0-1 History ho-hum. You're more interested in making history than studying it!

2-5 History honour roll. You're off to a historic start!

6-8 History home run. You sure know a lot about the olden days for a kid!

9-11 History hero! And future history professor!

What in the World Is . . . ?

Can you match these famous Canadian landmarks to the incomplete images below?

Banff, Château Frontenac, CN Tower, Confederation Bridge, Hopewell Rocks, Niagara Falls, Parliament Buildings, Science World Vancouver

1.

2.

3.

4.

5.

6.

7.

8.

45

SCORING

Give yourself one maple leaf for each correct answer.

1. Niagara Falls
2. Hopewell Rocks
3. Confederation Bridge
4. CN Tower
5. Château Frontenac
6. Banff
7. Parliament Buildings
8. Science World
   Vancouver

HOW YOU RATE . . .

0-1 Out of sight, out of mind. And out of gas.

2-4 Seeing is believing. Perhaps you'll see all of these landmarks in person one day!

5-8 See and be seen. Because you're the star of this scene!

How Weird Is Canada?

Canada has some very weird stuff. Super weird. Can you tell which freaky facts are true and which are bogus? Answer true or false to each question.

1. Canada geese speak many different languages.
2. Narcisse, Manitoba, is the home of the largest snake dens in the world.
3. You can drink a beverage in Dawson City, Yukon, that has a real human toe in it!
4. The Stanley Cup has its own bodyguard.
5. Canada has more doughnut shops per capita than any other country.
6. A Canadian once held the world record for balancing the most spoons on the face.
7. The city of Nanaimo, British Columbia, holds an annual bathtub race.
8. Canadians consume 10.6 kilograms of cheddar cheese a year. EACH.
9. There are more than 20 active volcanoes in Canada.
10. Canada's tallest trees measure more than 95 metres tall.
11. There are 55,000 different species of insects in Canada.
12. When extraterrestrials come to Earth for a visit, they will find a UFO landing pad waiting for them in St. Paul, Alberta.
13. In Churchill, Manitoba, there's a prison for polar bears.
14. A Canadian coin — a special edition quarter — features a glow-in-the-dark dinosaur.
15. Canadians are so fond of saying, "I'm sorry," there is an official law called the "Apology Act."

SCORING

Surprise! Every freaky fact is true! Give yourself one point for each correct answer.

1. True. The geese speak as many as 13 distinct dialects!
2. True. As many as 70,000 snakes hibernate there each winter in huge slithery serpent balls. They come out all at once in May.
3. True. It's called a Sourtoe cocktail.
4. True. It actually has four of them.
5. True. The most popular Canadian doughnut is the apple fritter.
6. True. It was 17.
7. True. The race was founded in 1967, for Canada's 100th birthday.
8. True. Canada's least favourite cheese is reportedly asiago.
9. True. They are in British Columbia and the Yukon.
10. True. They are spruce trees located in Carmanah Walbran, British Columbia.
11. True.
12. True. It was built in 1967, to attract both tourists and Martians.
13. True. Polar bears that come too close to town and could be dangerous are taken there. They are later released far from the town.
14. True.
15. True.

HOW YOU RATE . . .

0-5 Wowed by the weirdness: Admit it, Canada's a lot weirder than you thought.
6-10 Weirdly average. Which makes you, in a weird way, one hundred percent Canadian.
11-15 Welcome to weird world! Congratulations! You are the prime minister of Weird!

The Maple Leaf Olympics

Terry Fox was a Canadian athlete who lost one leg to cancer. In 1980, as a way to inspire people and to raise money for cancer research, he decided to run from coast to coast.

Since then, the Terry Fox Run has become an annual fundraising event. Across the country, millions of people participate in fun runs every year, and millions of dollars have been raised for a worthy cause.

Want to participate? Look for a Terry Fox Run in your community and sign up! Until then, compete in the Maple Leaf Olympics, both for lots of giggles and to see how much "money" you can raise for charity! Grab a friend to hold the stopwatch and say, "Ready, set, go." (Don't forget to give them a turn too.) Compete against your own best scores, or against each other. Make up your own wacky challenges for even more fun.

Maple Leaf Jump

You will need:
- sidewalk chalk
- a stopwatch or timer

Instructions:
Using the chalk, draw a maple leaf on the sidewalk. The leaf shape should measure about 80 cm across, or a distance that you can jump from a point on the left to a point on the right easily (but not too easily!).

Your challenge: Starting at the stem, jump to any point on the leaf. Then jump to any other point. If you make a mistake or step off the leaf, start over!

Your challenge is to complete all 11 jumps in as short a time as possible.

Ice Floe Hop Race

You will need:

- a flat piece of ground without any obstacles
- a stopwatch or timer

Instructions:

Decide on a starting line and a finish line. On *Go!*, hop on one foot onto an imaginary ice floe, then hop to the next one on the other foot, and hop to the next one on both feet. Repeat the sequence until you reach the finish line. If you mess up the steps or fall over (into the freezing cold water!), you must go back to the starting line.

Your challenge is to get to the finish line in as short a time as possible.

Sourtoe Tricks

You will need:

- 20 small pebbles or plastic toys of irregular shape
- a bowl or container
- a stopwatch or timer

Instructions:

Scatter the pebbles in a circle at your feet. Place the container on the floor beside them. Using your toes, pick up each of the pebbles, one at a time, and deposit it in the container. Extra points if you can get them all into the container without holding on to anything, falling over or putting your foot completely down on the ground.

You're not done yet: Empty the container and repeat the tricky toe challenge with the other foot!

Your challenge is to complete the task in as short a time as possible.

The Queen's Throne Challenge

You will need:
- a wall
- a stopwatch or timer

Instructions:
Stand against the wall with your feet about 15 cm away from it.

Bend your knees and slide down the wall until you are in a sitting position as shown, on an imaginary royal throne. Adjust your feet so they are firmly planted.

Hold this position for as long as you can. It's harder than it looks!

Your challenge is to hold this position for as long as possible.

Rolling Across the Prairies Challenge

You will need:
- a flat, unobstructed grassy area
- a stopwatch or timer

Instructions:
Decide on a starting line. Make sure there are no obstacles in any direction.

Do as many forward rolls as you can in 30 seconds.

Repeat — and beat your previous score — for a "round" of applause and a win!

START

SCORING

Give yourself one point for each challenge you completed.

HOW YOU RATE . . .

1. Bronze level fundraiser. You have raised $10,000 for a charity of your choice — and bought team uniforms for a kids' sports league.

2. Silver level fundraiser. You've raised $50,000 and funded an entire school sports program!

3. Gold level fundraiser. You have raised $100,000 and funded a summer sports program for 100 kids!

4. Platinum level fundraiser. You've raised enough money to fund the Canadian junior hockey team at next year's World Championship!

5. Philanthropist of the year! You have raised $1,000,000 for a charity of your choice and been named a national icon!

Are You Ready for Prime (Ministers) Time?

How much do you know about Canada's system of government and our leaders? Will you be elected "Leader in Knowledge" or sent to the backbench?

1. Canada's style of government is called . . .
   a. parliamentary democracy.
   b. republican monarchy.
   c. constitutional parliament.
2. Canada was founded in . . .
   a. 1857.
   b. 1867.
   c. 1887.
3. What were Canada's four founding provinces?
   a. Manitoba, Ontario, Quebec, New Brunswick.
   b. Ontario, Quebec, New Brunswick, Newfoundland.
   c. Ontario, Quebec, Nova Scotia, New Brunswick.
4. Canada's first prime minister was . . .
   a. William Lyon Mackenzie.
   b. Mackenzie King.
   c. John A. Macdonald.
5. The queen or king of England is Canada's official . . .
   a. prime minister.
   b. governor general.
   c. head of state.

6. True or false: There has never been a female prime minister in Canada.
7. The prime minister's closest advisors are called . . .
   a. the Cabinet.
   b. the Council.
   c. the Crew.
8. Which prime minister is shown on the Canadian five-dollar bill?
   a. Pierre Trudeau.
   b. Wilfrid Laurier.
   c. Stephen Harper.
9. Which prime minister held seances to talk to his dead dog?
   a. William Lyon Mackenzie King.
   b. Lester B. Pearson.
   c. Louis St-Laurent.
10. Which prime minister never attended school?
    a. Justin Trudeau.
    b. John A. Macdonald.
    c. Robert Borden.

SCORING

Give yourself one point for each correct answer.

1. a	3. c	5. c	7. a	9. a
2. b	4. c	6. False	8. b	10. c

HOW YOU RATE . . .

0-1 Out of office. Good luck in your next election!

2-6 On the ballot. You have a chance of getting a seat in Parliament.

7-10 Party leader. In the next election, you may become PM!

Made in Canada

Canadians are a very inventive people! Which of these famous inventions were devised in Canada?

canola oil	Aspirin	skis	peanut butter	insulin	zipper	hair transplants	frozen food
lighter	walkie-talkie	telegraph	dog collar	yo-yo	electric wheelchair	banana split	basketball
shoelace	flannel	fishing pole	highlighter	snowmobile	LED light	combustion engine	hard cup jockstrap
baseball	ice cream	helicopter	camp stove	electric oven	screen door	hammock	microphone
scissors	back scratcher	paint roller	Rollerblades	sauna	toboggan	s'more	sonar
AM radio	shoehorn	wind turbine	sash window	snow blower	solar panel	foghorn	radar
three-hole punch	ice skates	electron microscope	cardiac pacemaker	bicycle	kayak	Morse code	telephone
green garbage bags	Styrofoam	steam engine	paper made from wood pulp	hot-air balloon	tape dispenser	caulking gun	reindeer repellant

SCORING

Give yourself one point for each correctly identified answer (22 max).

Canola oil, peanut butter, insulin, zipper, walkie-talkie, electric wheelchair, basketball, snowmobile, hard cup jockstrap, electric oven, paint roller, toboggan, AM radio, snow blower, foghorn, electron microscope, cardiac pacemaker, kayak, telephone, green garbage bags, paper made from wood pulp, caulking gun.

Take away one point for each incorrect answer you selected (42 max).

Aspirin, skis, hair transplants, frozen food, lighter, telegraph, dog collar, yo-yo, banana split, shoelace, flannel, fishing pole, highlighter,

LED light, combustion engine, baseball, ice cream, helicopter, camp stove, screen door, hammock, microphone, scissors, back scratcher, Rollerblades, sauna, s'more, sonar, shoehorn, wind turbine, sash window, solar panel, radar, three-hole punch, ice skates, bicycle, Morse code, Styrofoam, steam engine, hot-air balloon, tape dispenser, reindeer repellant.

HOW YOU RATE...

-42-0 Australian invention expert! You probably know more about the land "down under" than the land "on top"!

1-5 PEI pro! You are on a first-name basis with some of Canada's greatest inventions.

6-12 Manitoba maven! You clearly have the inside track on Canada's inventive history.

13-19 Alberta ace! You get an A on the Made in Canada quiz!

20-22 Saskatchewan star! You have potential to become Canada's next great inventor.

For Loons Only!

1. A monster ate the Canadian prime minister! What time is it?
   a. Eight PM
   b. Midnight
   c. Eight a.m.
2. What do you get when you cross a great hockey player and a plumber?
   a. Blobby Orr.
   b. Sinkney Crosby.
   c. Drain Gretzky.
3. Why are Canadian students so smart?
   a. They're the tops in North America.
   b. They get a lot of ehs.
   c. Because Canada ends with an A.
4. Who wrote *My Mitten Got Eaten*?
   a. I.C. Fingers.
   b. Margaret Atwood.
   c. Robert Munsch.
5. What Canadian animal has antlers and sucks blood?
   a. A vampire reindeer.
   b. A *moose*quito.
   c. A cariblood.
6. What did the big furry hat say to the warm woolly scarf?
   a. "You hang around; I'll go on ahead."
   b. "Don't you just love summer in Moose Jaw?"
   c. "Watch out. Robert Munsch ate our pal Mittens!"
7. Why didn't the tourist in Canada get any sleep?
   a. She kept waiting for the sun to set. In July. In Nunavut.
   b. He plugged his electric blanket into the toaster by mistake and kept popping out of bed all night!
   c. Because Canada is the most exciting country on earth!

8. What happened when all the muskox wool in Canada was stolen?
   a. There was a very hairy police chase!
   b. The muskox got cold ankles.
   c. The police combed the area.
9. What do you call ten Arctic hares hopping backwards through the snow together?
   a. Tuesday in Canada.
   b. A receding hare line.
   c. Bieber bunnies.
10. What do Canadian snowmen call their offspring?
   a. Icikids.
   b. Snowballs.
   c. *Chill*dren.

SCORING

1. a5 b3 c1	3. a5 b3 c1	5. a3 b5 c1	7. a1 b5 c3	9. a1 b5 c3
2. a3 b5 c1	4. a5 b3 c1	6. a5 b1 c3	8. a3 b1 c5	10. a1 b3 c5

HOW YOU RATE . . .

10-20 Northern nope. You were just joking, right?

21-30 Sit down comic. You succeed at silliness!

31-40 Canadian comedian. You're almost ready for late night TV!

41-50 You're so punny! And the Funniest Kid in Canada!

For Canuckleheads Only!

1. How do Canadians get to work?
   a. By icicle.
   b. Jet skis.
   c. Snowflake wagons.
2. How do Canadians greet each other?
   a. Nice weather, eh?
   b. Ice to meet you!
   c. Nice to see you again!

3. What do you call a Canadian T. Rex?
   a. Extinct.
   b. A coldasaurus.
   c. A dinosorry.
4. What do they decorate cakes with up north?
   a. Permafrosting.
   b. Icing.
   c. Porcupine quills.
5. What did the beaver say to the maple tree?
   a. "It's been nice gnawing you."
   b. "Is your favourite hockey team the Leafs?"
   c. "Mind if I log on?"
6. What's Canada's favourite dessert?
   a. Chocolate moose.
   b. Cookie doe ice cream.
   c. Blue*beary* pie.
7. What do Canadians put on their hot dogs?
   a. Snow caps.
   b. *Moose*tard.
   c. Sled harnesses.

8. What are polar bears' favourite snacks?
   a. Fish sticks.
   b. Goldfish crackers.
   c. *Brrrr*itos.
9. Knock, knock! Who's there?
   a. Sorry. No, I'm sorry. No, I'm sorry.
   b. Tuque. Tuque who? Tuque you by surprise, didn't I?
   c. Yukon. Yukon who? Yukon open the door any time now!
10. Where in Canada are you most likely to meet a Bigfoot?
    a. Biggar, Saskatchewan.
    b. Hairy Hill, Alberta.
    c. *Sasquatch*ewan.

SCORING

1. a5 b3 c1	3. a3 b1 c5	5. a5 b1 c3	7. a3 b5 c1	9. a5 b3 c1
2. a3 b5 c2	4. a5 b3 c1	6. a5 b2 c3	8. a1 b3 c5	10. a1 b3 c5

HOW YOU RATE . . .

12-20 Fungi. You are a pretty fun guy or gal.
21-30 Funder and lightning. You make others laugh up a storm.
31-40 Funky! You've got the key to Canadian humour.
41-50 Funster! You really stir up the laughs!

Canada Counts!

Do your Canadian math skills add up?

1. Multiply the number of provinces by the number of territories.
2. How much maple syrup is in the jug?
   a. 750 metres
   b. 750 millimetres
   c. 750 millilitres
3. Subtract the number of goals in a hat trick from the number of Canadian NHL teams.
4. If you add a Canadian nickel, dime, quarter, loonie and toonie together, how much money do you have?
5. How many rectangles can you make using the lines on the Canadian flag (not counting the lines in the leaf design)?

6. How long is this ski?
   a. 1 metre
   b. 1,000 millimetres
   c. Both a and b
7. Subtract the house number of the prime minister's official residence from the total number of MPs in Canada's Parliament.
8. What is this hockey stick's perimeter?

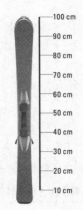

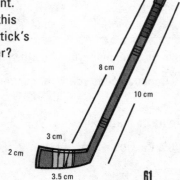

9. Which animal has the largest population in Canada?
   a. Beluga whale.
   b. Moose.
   c. Grizzly bear.
10. What fraction of this sugar pie has been eaten by the wolverine?
   a. 3/8
   b. 5/8
   c. 3/5

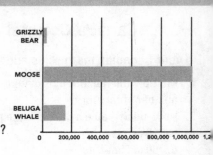

SCORING

Give yourself ten points for each correct answer.

1. 30. There are ten provinces and three territories.
2. c
3. 4. There are three goals in a hat trick and seven Canadian NHL teams.
4. $3.40
5. 6
6. c
7. 314. There are 338 Members of Parliament, and the PM lives at 24 Sussex Drive.
8. 27.5 cm
9. b
10. a

HOW YOU RATE . . .

0-10 Zzzzz student. Have you been sleeping through math class?

20-50 C student. Don't fret — Canada needs you. Without you, we would be Anada.

60-90 B student. You measure up on math skills.

100 Eh! student. You are a 100% Canadian math whiz.

Whirl-a-Word

Oh no! These all-Canadian words have gone through the Blizzard Blender. Can you unscramble them?

1. IOTPNUE
2. SUNIKUK
3. ULAWRS
4. TNEMAILRAP
5. YAAKK
6. YAGACLR
7. SCALROSE
8. YONKU
9. KEDNOKLI
10. GOPOGOO

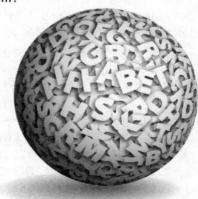

SCORING

Give yourself ten points for each correct answer.

1. poutine	4. Parliament	7. lacrosse	9. Klondike
2. inuksuk	5. kayak	8. Yukon	10. Ogopogo
3. walrus	6. Calgary		

HOW YOU RATE . . .

0-30 TON OOT DAB! (Not too bad!)

40-70 PTEYRT OGOD! (Pretty good!)

80-100 SPUER KUNCCA! (Super Canuck!)

Canada's Best Spy Agent — You!

Can you decode this top-secret Canadian code and save the country from our worst enemies? Choose one of the two possible code keys to use. Then substitute the matching letter for each number in the coded message. Canada depends on you!

1. 14 22 22 7 2 12 6 9 24 12 13 7 26 24 7 18 13 25 9 26 14 11 7 12 13 26 7 13 12 12 13.

2. 7 19 22 9 22 18 8 26 13 22 13 22 14 2 11 12 15 26 9 25 22 26 9 18 13 7 19 22 9 22 21 9 18 20 22 9 26 7 12 9. 23 18 8 26 9 14 19 22 9.

3. 7 5 20 6 9 18 5 4 21 16! 25 15 21 18 3 15 14 20 1 3 20 9 19 4 9 19 7 21 9 19 5 4 1 19 1 3 1 12 7 1 18 25 6 12 1 1 13 5.

4. 2 12 6 26 9 22 13 22 22 23 22 23 26 7 24 26 14 11 3. 23 22 11 26 9 7 18 14 14 22 23 18 26 7 22 15 2.

5. 20 8 5 19 5 3 18 5 20 3 15 4 5 23 15 18 4 9 19 "22 15 25 1 7 5 21 18."

Code Key #1

A	B	C	D	E	F	G	H	I
1	2	3	4	5	6	7	8	9
J	K	L	M	N	O	P	Q	R
10	11	12	13	14	15	16	17	18
S	T	U	V	W	X	Y	Z	
19	20	21	22	23	24	25	26	

Code Key #2

A	B	C	D	E	F	G	H	I
26	25	24	23	22	21	20	19	18
J	K	L	M	N	O	P	Q	R
17	16	15	14	13	12	11	10	9
S	T	U	V	W	X	Y	Z	
8	7	6	5	4	3	2	1	

SCORING

Give yourself one very secret point for each message you successfully decoded.

1. Use code key #2 to get: Meet your contact in Brampton at noon.
2. Use code key #2 to get: There is an enemy polar bear in the refrigerator. Disarm her.
3. Use code key #1 to get: Get fired up! Your contact is disguised as a Calgary Flame.
4. Use code key #2 to get: You are needed at Camp X. Depart immediately.
5. Use code key #1 to get: The secret code word is "voyageur."

HOW YOU RATE . . .

1-2 Undercover expert. Stay in bed.

3-4 Case officer. You better watch behind you, just in case!

5 Canadian spymaster. 3 1 14 1 4 1 20 8 1 14 11 19   25 15 21! (Canada thanks you!)

Extreme Canada

Highest, coldest, biggest, fastest — test your knowledge of Canada's record holders. Do you come up short or out on top?

1. What is Canada's highest mountain?
   a. Mount Logan.
   b. Denali.
   c. Mount Everest.
2. What is Canada's coldest recorded temperature?
   a. -44°C.
   b. -63°C.
   c. -5°C.
3. What is Canada's deepest lake?
   a. Great Slave Lake.
   b. Great Bear Lake.
   c. Lake Superior.
4. What is the largest lake that lies completely within Canada?
   a. Great Slave Lake.
   b. Great Bear Lake.
   c. Lake Superior.
5. What is the fastest Canadian land animal?
   a. The cougar.
   b. The muskox.
   c. The pronghorn.
6. Which is the largest Canadian land animal?
   a. The wood bison.
   b. The Canadian elephant.
   c. The moose.
7. What is the rarest Canadian animal?
   a. The beluga whale.
   b. The Vancouver Island marmot.
   c. The polar bear.

8. Toronto is Canada's largest city. Which city is the second largest?
   a. Vancouver.
   b. Calgary.
   c. Montreal.
9. Greenwood, British Columbia, is Canada's smallest city. How many people call it home?
   a. Less than 10.
   b. Less than 500.
   c. Less than 1,000.
10. What is Canada's — and the world's — northernmost settlement?
    a. Alert, Nunavut.
    b. Grise Fjord, Nunavut.
    c. Resolute, Nunavut.
11. What is the rainiest province in Canada?
    a. British Columbia.
    b. Nova Scotia.
    c. New Brunswick.
12. How long is the longest night in Canada?
    a. 6 hours.
    b. 16 hours.
    c. Several months.

SCORING

Give yourself five points for each correct answer.

1. a. It measures 5,959 m tall.
2. b. It was recorded in Snag, Yukon, on February 3, 1947.
3. a. It measures 614 m deep.
4. b. Lake Superior is larger, but part of it lies inside the United States.
5. c. It can run up to 72 km per hour.
6. a. Adult males can reach up to 3.8 m in length, measure 2 m in height at the shoulder and weigh up to 900 kg.
7. b. There are fewer than 300 Vancouver Island marmots in the wild.
8. c. It has over 1.6 million residents.
9. c. It has about 700 residents.
10. a. It is located at latitude N 82°30'05", 817 km from the North Pole.
11. a. The rainiest place in Canada is Moresby Island, British Columbia. It gets 6,325 mm of rain every year.
12. c. North of the Arctic Circle, Canada experiences polar night. The sun will not rise above the horizon for months!

HOW YOU RATE . . .

0-15 Canada's randomest guesser. You excel at growing long fingernails.

20-45 Canada's cleverest figure-it-outer. You're tops at doing quizzes.

50-60 Canada's extreme quiz champ! You're the fastest at sneaking peeks at the quiz answers.

Would You Survive as a Voyageur?

You are a voyageur working for the Hudson's Bay Company, travelling hundreds of kilometres into Canada's interior and buying furs to trade. Which path will you take — and more importantly, will you survive the journey?

1. Your canoe route will take you through the mosquito-filled swamps to Kenora, or the blackfly-riddled bogs to Fort Frances. Which route will you take?
   a. The route to Kenora. > Go to question 2.
   b. The route to Fort Frances > Go to question 3.

2. On your first day you need to do a 10 km portage through a mosquito-filled swamp. You . . .
   a. heft your canoe over your head and sing your favourite song, "En roulant ma boule," at the top of your lungs. > Go to question 4.
   b. catch as many mosquitoes as you can and save them to roast for dinner. Mosquito pie makes good eating. > Go to question 5.

3. Your fellow voyageurs seem shifty. You . . .
   a. try to make friends. > Go to question 17.
   b. keep to yourself. > Go to question 18.

4. The next morning starts out fine, but by lunchtime rain is pouring down. You . . .
   a. alternate between paddling and bailing out your canoe. > Go to question 6.
   b. start splashing your travelling companions in the lead canoe with your paddle. > Go to question 7.

5. The second day of your trip takes you through some serious whitewater. You ...
   a. paddle furiously. > Go to question 10.
   b. hold your paddle steady to steer better. > Go to question 11.

6. Time to make camp! You ...
   a. choose a spot next to a scenic waterfall. Fat salmon swim at its base. > Go to question 8.
   b. decide to camp in a dry cave a few hundred metres away from the river. > Go to question 9.

7. The water fight turns into an epic battle. You send tidal waves of water at the lead canoe. > The canoe tips and the leader of the expedition is furious. For the rest of your journey, you have to carry the heaviest canoes, make fires with the wettest wood and sleep on the lumpiest part of the ground. You don't mind though — that water fight was so much fun, it was all worth it. YOU SURVIVE THE JOURNEY.

8. The fish swimming in the pool attract another visitor — a very hungry bear! You ...
   a. fight the bear for the fish. > You win. Not only do you have a delicious supper, but you have collected a mighty nice fur for trading. YOU SURVIVE THE JOURNEY.
   b. hide. > The bear was very, very hungry. But now that it has eaten its fill, it turns out to be very friendly and an excellent guide. The bear leads you to a trading post where you collect the finest furs you've ever seen with no difficulty whatsoever. You return to Montreal in no time, sell your furs and make the trip to your secret trading post twelve more times, then retire a very wealthy person. YOU SURVIVE THE JOURNEY.

9. The cave is dark. You . . .
   a. step inside. > Go to question 15.
   b. toss a rock inside to see if anything stirs. > Go to question 16.

10. You get through the rapids and decide to camp beside a tall pine tree. You set up . . .
    a. your shelter. > Go to question 12.
    b. your cooking fire. > Go to question 13.

11. Your canoe tips! You kick your feet and struggle to get your head above water. You spot a log floating past to your right and, farther away, the branch of a tree reaching into the water. You . . .
    a. paddle hard and head toward the branch. > You feel something brush against your leg. It's a magical salmon. It nudges you out of the water so you can breathe. Then it carries you on its back all the way to Kenora. YOU SURVIVE THE JOURNEY, but you have to avoid eating seafood for the rest of your life.
    b. grab onto the log. > Go to question 14.

12. A baby bear has been clinging to the tree above your head. The bear is so cute! You . . .
    a. try to coax the cute little cub out of the tree. > You turn around and discover mama bear is right behind you! You try to scramble away, but the bear is not amused. She bats you out of her way with her huge paw, removing half of your hair. She climbs the tree and collects her cub, and when she passes you again, she gives you a haughty look and kicks some dirt in your face. When she is gone, you brush off your face, fix your hair and finish making camp. > YOU SURVIVE THE JOURNEY.
    b. run! You know this means trouble. > Go to question 23.

13. A family of porcupines is clinging to the tree above your head. Porcupines smell really bad, but they really don't bother you in any other way. You finish cooking, tamp down your fire and go to bed. You sleep like a baby. In the morning, you discover the trading post you were aiming for is on the other side of the river. Now that was easy! > YOU SURVIVE THE JOURNEY.

14. You haul yourself out of the water, bruised and exhausted. That was FUN! You continue your journey and spend the rest of your life as a very happy and very lucky voyageur. > YOU SURVIVE THE JOURNEY.

15. You discover a bear snoring inside! You . . .
    a. back out of the cave, leaving the bear in dreamland. > But while you were gone, the rest of your crew has disappeared. Rather than sleep all alone in the woods, you return to your canoe, paddle another 10 km and arrive at a sparkling creek near dawn. You discover that the creek is sparkling because it is filled with gold. You find your pals (they really love you now!), collect several kilograms of the stuff, paddle back to Montreal and retire a wealthy person. YOU SURVIVE THE JOURNEY.
    b. wake the bear to chase it out of the cave. > The bear is not amused. You have an epic fight. The story of this fight becomes a very famous legend that is told around voyageur campfires to this day. Alas, your life does not last quite as long as the legend. The bear eats you for supper and then — *burp!* — goes back to a peaceful sleep. JOURNEY JOKE.

16. There are roosting bats inside! They come flying out at you! You . . .

a. bed down for the night and continue your journey in the morning. Bats don't bother you! > Go to question 3.

b. run away from the cave. Bats terrify you! > But it's dark out, and you weren't paying attention, and you now have no idea where you are or where your canoe is. You spend a miserable night in the woods, cold, wet and determined to give up this crazy career. JOURNEY JOKE.

17. You discover that your fellow voyageurs are actually pirates who have decided to give up the sea. You . . .

a. brag about how you once met Bluebeard, the famous French pirate. > Go to question 19.

b. gulp nervously. > Go to question 20.

18. It turns out that all your fellow voyageurs have the beginning symptoms of a terrible disease. When you wake up in the morning, you discover they have all died during the night! Because you kept to yourself, you do not catch it. That's a relief! But now you are all alone in the wilderness. Luckily, you know how to paddle a canoe, you have warm clothes, plenty of food, hunting equipment and a map to follow. You make it to the trading post in one piece, join a new group of voyageurs heading east and return to Montreal with a canoe full of furs. > YOU SURVIVE THE JOURNEY.

19. One fellow announces he knows you are a liar, because *he* is Bluebeard. You scream in terror. He laughs in your face and twirls the hairs in his very blue beard. So sorry, your days — er, minutes — are numbered. > JOURNEY JOKE.

20. They laugh. One of the fellows shouts, "Really had you going there, didn't we!" You are so embarrassed! You . . .
    a. blush furiously. > Go to question 21.
    b. shout, "Well, you are mean enough to be pirates!" > Go to question 22.

21. Your fellow voyageurs slap you on the back and welcome you to their group. > YOU SURVIVE THE JOURNEY.

22. Your fellow voyageurs look *soooo* sad. The big one, the one with the blue beard, even starts to cry. They didn't mean to hurt your feelings! They're just a rough bunch, after all, without much in the way of manners. Will you ever forgive them? You do. > YOU SURVIVE THE JOURNEY.

23. You make so much noise crashing through the brush that some local folks hear you. They come to your rescue. They feed you and give you a nice toasty place to sleep by the fire. You become trading partners and live happily ever after. > YOU SURVIVE THE JOURNEY.

What Iconic Canadian Animal Are You?

Are you mischievous, like a raccoon, or do you prefer to take a bird's-eye view, like a blue jay? What Canadian animal best matches up with your quirky Canadian personality?

1. Which would be your preferred view out your bedroom window?
   a. A stunning beach. > Got to question 2.
   b. A woodland scene. > Go to question 3.
   c. A cityscape. > Go to question 4.
2. Which do you prefer?
   a. Playing tag. > Go to question 5.
   b. Playing dodge ball. > Go to question 6.
3. People see you as . . .
   a. bright and responsible. > Go to question 7.
   b. fun loving and lighthearted. > Go to question 8.
4. You prefer . . .
   a. solid colours. > You are a POLAR BEAR.
   b. interesting patterns. > You are an ORCA.
5. People think you are . . .
   a. outgoing and goofy. > You are a BELUGA WHALE.
   b. private and mysterious. > You are a WALRUS.
6. You would rather eat . . .
   a. a veggie kabob. > You are a BEAVER.
   b. a bison burger. > You are a LYNX.
7. You are secretly . . .
   a. shyer than people think. > You are a PORCUPINE.
   b. more of a risk taker than people think. > You are a MOOSE.

8. You prefer . . .
   a. diamonds. > Go to question 9.
   b. gold. > Go to question 10.
9. You are . . .
   a. an early bird. > You are a
   BLUE JAY.
   b. a night owl. > You are a
   RACCOON.
10. You are . . .
   a. an omnivore — you love all kinds of food, no matter how
   exotic. > You are a SKUNK.
   b. a picky eater. > You are a SQUIRREL.

WHAT YOUR ANIMAL SAYS ABOUT YOU . . .

Beaver. You are a hard worker and very thoughtful — you like to chew things over before you make a decision. Future career: Architect. Favourite toy: LEGO,

Beluga whale. You are cheerful, playful and love to sing and dance. You have a super nice smile! You look good in white. Future career: Rock star. Favourite game: Hide-and-seek.

Blue jay. You are the life of the party! A bit bossy at times, but the world needs someone like you to take charge. You love sports, bright, shiny objects and learning new things. Future career: Prime minister. Favourite sport: Baseball.

Lynx. You are clever and good at making connections between ideas. You are great at spotting new opportunities and pouncing on them. Future career: IT professional. Favourite game: Mouse Trap.

Moose. People tend to notice you. Perhaps you need to bathe more? Or maybe it's your very large personality. You are easygoing, loyal and a bit loud. Try not to chew with your mouth open. Future career: NHL star. Favourite toy: Yo-yo.

Orca. You tend to see the world in black and white. You are very sociable and enjoy hanging out in groups. You have a biting sense of humour. Future career: Fashion designer. Favourite game: Checkers.

Polar bear. You like to go with the flow. You are cute and cuddly but can be terrifying when angry. When stressed, you respond by hitting the pause button. Future career: Bobsled racer. Favourite sport: Fishing.

Porcupine. You can be prickly at times, but have a very soft heart. You tend to keep to yourself, but pine for fame. Secretly, you are a real ham. Future career: Writer. Favourite toy: Pick-up sticks.

Raccoon. You are mischievous, good with your hands and too smart for your own good. You can be something of a smart aleck. Get more sleep — you have black circles around your eyes. Future career: Stockbroker. Favourite game: Clue.

Skunk. You have a great sense of style and a strong sense of self. You are sophisticated and mature, but watch out for your temper tantrums! They really stink. Future career: Broadcaster. Favourite game: Chess.

Squirrel. You are very restless and like to be active at all times. Sometimes you can be a bit nutty. You love telling tall tales. Future career: Professional gymnast. Favourite game: Tag.

Walrus. You love to hang out on a comfy couch, chilling. You have an artistic temperament and love to read. Other people might occasionally find you strange, but you know that you are beautiful both inside and out. Future career: Film director. Favourite activity: Napping.

Are You Ship Shape?

Canada is surrounded by ocean on three sides. Is your knowledge of Canadian waters seaworthy?

1. What ocean lies to the north of Canada?
   a. Atlantic Ocean.
   b. Pacific Ocean.
   c. Arctic Ocean.

2. Sea otters live along Canada's west coast. Which otter fact is NOT true?
   a. Sea otters are closely related to porpoises.
   b. Sea otters frequently hold hands when they sleep.
   c. Sea otters use rocks to smash open their favourite foods — shellfish.

3. How many different species of seals can you find in Canadian waters?
   a. 1.
   b. 6.
   c. 8.

4. What Canadian ocean animal can you find on the toonie?
   a. Beaver.
   b. Narwhal.
   c. Polar bear.

5. The Bay of Fundy is known for . . .
   a. the highest tides in the world.
   b. the warmest water in Canada.
   c. the most fun bodysurfing.
6. Which ocean borders Vancouver Island?
   a. Arctic Ocean.
   b. Pacific Ocean.
   c. Atlantic Ocean.
7. Which ocean is largest?
   a. Arctic Ocean.
   b. Pacific Ocean.
   c. Atlantic Ocean.
8. Which ocean animal from Canadian waters was a major source of food for Europeans for hundreds of years?
   a. Atlantic cod.
   b. American lobster.
   c. Pacific halibut.
9. Which body of water separates Vancouver Island from the mainland of Canada?
   a. Strait of Georgia.
   b. Northwest Passage.
   c. St. Lawrence Seaway.
10. What tiny sea animal is the major food source for humpback whales, bringing them to feeding grounds off Canada's coasts every summer?
    a. Cod.
    b. Seal.
    c. Krill.

SCORING:

Give yourself four points for each correct answer.

1. c	3. b	5. a	7. b	9. a
2. a	4. c	6. b	8. a	10. c

HOW YOU RATE . . .

0-8 Sea you later! You are a born landlubber.

12-28 Anchors away! You've begun the journey to ocean expertise.

32-40 Deep knowledge. You are Captain Canada!

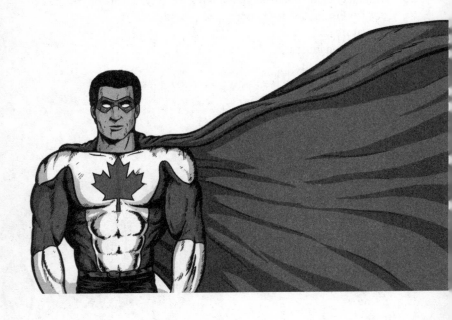

Book a Trip to Canada!

Canada has the greatest kids' books in the world. How well do you know these Canadian books, authors and characters?

1. What charming Canadian critter is extremely shy and nervous?
   a. Silverwing.
   b. Tigger.
   c. Scaredy Squirrel.

2. A. A. Milne wrote the famous books about Winnie the Pooh based on a real bear cub, which was named after what Canadian city?
   a. Winnipeg.
   b. Winn's Falls.
   c. Windermere.

3. Anne Shirley lived on what Canadian island?
   a. Vancouver Island.
   b. Prince Edward Island.
   c. Baffin Island.

4. What kind of animal is Silverwing?
   a. A blue jay.
   b. A bat.
   c. A snowy owl.

5. What famous Canadian author wrote a poem about a pie made from alligators?
   a. Robert Munsch.
   b. Helaine Becker.
   c. Dennis Lee.

6. What kind of animal is Franklin?
   a. A turtle.
   b. A dog.
   c. A cat.

7. Which of the following books did Robert Munsch NOT write?
   a. *The Paper Bag Princess*.
   b. *A Porcupine in a Pine Tree*.
   c. *Smelly Socks*.
8. What shape is Caillou's head?
   a. Square like a block.
   b. Round like a lollipop.
   c. He doesn't have a head.
9. What famous Canadian artist illustrates her books with Plasticine?
   a. Frieda Wishinsky.
   b. Paulette Bourgeois.
   c. Barbara Reid.

10. What colour is best?
    a. Red.
    b. Blue.
    c. Pink.

SCORING

Give yourself one point for each correct answer.

1. c	3. b	5. c	7. b	9. c
2. a	4. b	6. a	8. b	10. a

HOW YOU RATE . . .

0-2 Book your travel tickets now! You have hours of fun reading and discovery ahead of you!

3-5 Your dream trip is booked! And of course your bag is packed with great Canadian books! Keep reading for even more fun.

6-10 You're at the gateway to adventure — travel book in hand! Canadian books take you places that are out of this world!

What Extremely Delicious Canadian Food Are You?

Sweet or spicy? Cool as a cucumber or stuffed full of love? Which Canadian delicacy best suits your stomach — and your unique personality?

1. People call you . . .
   a. sweet. > Go to question 2.
   b. trouble! > Go to question 3.
   c. friendly. > Go to question 4.
2. You prefer . . .
   a. swimming. > Go to question 5.
   b. skiing. > Go to question 6.
3. You are a . . .
   a. morning person. > You are BANNOCK.
   b. night owl. > You are POUTINE.
4. You prefer . . .
   a. drawing dogs. > You are SUGAR PIE.
   b. riding horses. > You are LOBSTER ROLLS.
5. You are more scared of . . .
   a. vampires. > You are BEAVER TAILS.
   b. ghosts. > You are MAPLE SYRUP.
6. You think carrots are . . .
   a. excellent for making snowman noses. > You are BUTTER TARTS.
   b. delicious. > You are NANAIMO BARS.

WHAT YOUR FOOD SAYS ABOUT YOU . . .

Bannock. You are warm and dependable. You like campfires and playing Nok Hockey.

Beaver Tails. You have a strong personality, but you can also be very sweet. Your favourite sport is ice skating. Don't forget to brush your teeth.

Butter tarts. You are very sentimental. You love cute kittens, fuzzy slippers and snowflakes that melt on your tongue. You hate it when people try to butter you up to get you to do something for them.

Lobster rolls. You can be crabby at times, but mostly you roll with the punches.

Maple syrup. You like to stick close to home, but you hate it when people leave without you.

Nanaimo bars. You are a person of many layers. You are an excellent speller. One day you will be famous.

Poutine. You are fun to be around. You tell cheesy jokes. You have a strange fondness for the Russian presidents.

Sugar pie (tarte au sucre). You seem very, very sweet, but you can also be quite tart. You would make a great secret agent — or dentist.

Could Albertosaurus Eat Your Homework?

What was Canada like in the time of the dinosaurs? And even before that? Dig deep into this quiz to see how much you know about Canada's prehistoric past.

1. Tiktaalik is the name of an extinct species of fish with a unique feature — it had legs! That means it was the first species of vertebrate that could leave the water. Where in Canada was it found?
   a. Downtown Toronto.
   b. Nunavut.
   c. Labrador.
2. Albertosaurus lived in western Canada and was related to T. Rex. When did it live?
   a. Before T. Rex.
   b. At the same time as T. Rex.
   c. After T. Rex.
3. The Burgess Shale, a fossil deposit in British Columbia, is a World Heritage Site because it has . . .
   a. unusually well-preserved mammoth and cave lion remains.
   b. a huge amount of some of the oldest fossils ever found.
   c. a large deposit of fossilized dinosaur eggs.

4. On Ontario's Manitoulin Island, you can readily spot fossils of sea creatures embedded in the rocks. How did they get there?
   a. A giant tidal wave once swept across Canada and deposited many dead animals across the landscape.
   b. A giant hurricane swept them up into the air and they rained down on the countryside.
   c. Oceans once covered large parts of central Canada.

5. At the World Heritage Site at Joggins, Nova Scotia, what incredible fossils can you see in the cliffs?
   a. Remains of giant trees.
   b. Preserved footprints of tetrapods.
   c. Both a and b.
6. True or false: Dire wolves once lived in Canada.
7. Which statement is true:
   a. Humans lived at the time of dinosaurs.
   b. Humans may have caused the extinction of the mammoth.
   c. Neither mammoths nor dinosaurs ever lived in Canada.

8. Where is the "Dinosaur Capital of the World"?
   a. Drumheller, Alberta.
   b. Trextown, Nova Scotia.
   c. Badlands, Manitoba.
9. Where in Canada can you go on a real dig and maybe find undiscovered fossils?
   a. Morden, Manitoba. Home to the Canadian Fossil Discovery Centre.
   b. There's no place like that in Canada.
   c. The Edmonton Mall.
10. True or false: A teenager found Canada's first discovered dinosaur nesting site at a place called Devil's Coulee, in Alberta.

11. A treasure trove of Canadian dinosaur bones was lost when . . .
    a. the famous dinosaur hunter Charles H. Sternberg died without providing their location in Alberta's badlands.
    b. the ship taking them to England was sunk by a German warship during World War I.
    c. the fossils were stolen from the Royal Tyrrell Museum in 1976.
12. Lambeosaurus, a species of duck-billed dinosaur, was named after . . .
    a. Lambton County, Ontario, where it was found.
    b. the Latin word *lambo*, which means "bill."
    c. Lawrence Lambe, a Canadian paleontologist.

SCORING

Give yourself one point for each correct answer.

1. b	3. b	5. c	7. b	9. a	11. b
2. a	4. c	6. True	8. a	10. True	12. c

HOW YOU RATE . . .

0-1 Precambrian kid. You are at the earliest era of knowledge on this subject.

2-6 Triassic kid. Keep trying, and before long you will be a qualified dino hunter!

7-9 Cretaceous kid. You are reaching the upper levels of prehistoric knowledge.

10-12 Certified paleontologist. You are a Canadian fossil expert!

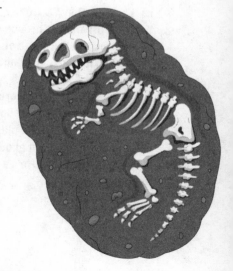

Would You Triumph as a Backcountry Flying Ace?

During the early days of aviation, Canadian bush pilots engaged in incredible acts of derring-do. How would you have fared as a bush pilot in the 1920s?

1. You head out to the airfield to check on your plane. As you're looking it over, your buddy, Billy Bishop, comes running over. He says, "There's a baby on the way in Wawa, and a fire in Hot Springs!" You say . . .

   a. "Hot dog! Hot Springs is ablaze!" > Go to question 2.

   b. "Wawa, here I come!" > Go to question 14.

2. You say . . .

   a. "I'm on it!" > Go to question 3.

   b. "Let's go, Billy." > Go to question 4.

3. You take off and fly through gorgeous clear blue skies. About 25 km from Hot Springs, you notice the fuel gauge is showing "low." You left in such a hurry, you forgot to put more fuel in your plane's tanks! You . . .

   a. decide you better turn around. > Go to question 5.

   b. keep going toward Hot Springs. > Go to question 6.

4. You and Billy jump in the plane and fly to Hot Springs. But you and Billy have an argument about the flight path. You . . .

   a. take Billy's advice. He's a World War I flying ace, after all. > Go to question 7.

   b. stick to your guns. > Go to question 10.

5. You start to turn the plane around, but the engine sputters! Things are even worse than you thought. You need to save fuel. You decide to . . .

   a. jettison all the firefighting equipment you brought with you. > Go to question 9.

   b. climb as high as you can with the plane, then turn off the engines and glide all the way back. > Go to question 11.

6. It's Hot Springs! Burning to a crisp! You see a logging road heading into the flames and aim for it. You . . .

   a. land successfully on the road. > Go to question 12.

   b. have trouble with the landing. > Go to question 13.

7. Billy may be a flying ace, but he has a terrible sense of direction. You are now hopelessly lost. You . . .

   a. yell at Billy. > Go to question 8.

   b. sigh and look out the window, hoping to recognize a landmark in the endless sea of trees below. > Go to question 10.

8. Billy gets mad at you and yells back. You . . .

   a. keep arguing and forget to steer the plane. > Go to question 18.

   b. shrug your shoulders and look out the window. > Go to question 10.

   c. convince Billy you are right and he is wrong. > Go to question 19.

9. Unfortunately, you only brought a water pistol and it isn't enough to lighten the load. Your plane goes down in the deep woods near Mosquito Lake. Miraculously, you survive the crash, but then are carried off by giant mosquitoes and never seen again. > FLYING ACE FACE PLANT.

10. You see a plume of smoke to the southeast! It must be Hot Springs! You head for it and arrive just in time to put out the fire. > FLYING ACE PHENOM.

11. A daring manoeuvre! Incredibly, it works! You land back at your home airfield, safe and sound. But when you tell your buddy Billy Bishop what happened, he stares at you in disbelief. "Thanks to you," he says, "Hot Springs has burned to the ground and is now Nowhere Lake." > FLYING ACE FACE PLANT.

12. You grab your firefighting gear and run into the flames. You find everyone in Hot Springs is busy passing buckets of water to put out the flames. You . . .
    a. go back to your plane and take a much-needed nap. > FLYING ACE FACE PLANT.
    b. join in the bucket brigade. > You save the town! FLYING ACE PHENOM.

13. The plane is out of control! You try to steer, but it skids off the road and right into the fire! Luckily it skids right OVER the burning bits and smothers them, putting the fire out. > FLYING ACE PHENOM.

14. You arrive in Wawa and race to the home of the expectant mother. She and the baby are in trouble! You . . .
    a. roll up your sleeves to help deliver the baby. > Go to question 15.
    b. bundle up the expectant mother and get her onto your plane pronto! > Go to question 16.
15. You deliver the baby! It's a girl! She's healthy and so is the mom. And you are a hero. They decide to name the baby after you. > FLYING ACE PHENOM.
16. You fly as fast as you can toward the nearest hospital. The expectant mother cries out, "The baby is coming!" You . . .
    a. fly even faster. > Go to question 17.
    b. tie your plane's steering column with your scarf so it holds a steady course. > Go to question 15.
17. You manage to make it to a hospital just in time. The baby is safely delivered and the mother is healthy and happy. > FLYING ACE PHENOM.
18. The plane crashes. Oops. > FLYING ACE FACE PLANT.
19. Billy really was right. You don't arrive at Hot Springs until it has burned to the ground. > FLYING ACE FACE PLANT but at least the embers are perfect for making s'mores.

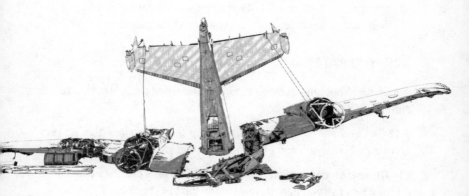

O Canada! Eh?

Most kids sing it every day at school. But not everyone fully knows what words they are singing. Can you fill in the blanks to complete the words of the anthem correctly?

_1_ Canada!
Our _2_ and _3_ land!
True patriot _4_ in all thy sons _5_.
With _6_ hearts we see thee rise,
The _7_ _8_ strong and _9_!
From far and wide
O Canada, we stand on _10_ for thee.
God keep our land _11_ and _12_!
O Canada, we stand on guard for thee.
O Canada, _13_ _14_ _15_ _16_ _17_ _18_.

SCORING:

Give yourself one point for each correct answer.

1. O	5. command	9. free	13. we	17. for
2. home	6. glowing	10. guard	14. stand	18. thee
3. native	7. True	11. glorious	15. on	
4. love	8. North	12. free	16. guard	

HOW YOU RATE ...

0-5 Oh my! You need some practice on the words, but feel free to hum along!

6-12 Oh goodie! You're the perfect singer for joining in with a large chorus (where everyone else knows all the words!).

13+ Oh boy, oh boy, oh boy! You're an "O Canada" pro! Are you warming up your pipes so you can perform at the next big hockey game?

Laura Secord Saves the Day — or Does She?

It is 1813, and you are a typical Canadian girl named Laura
Secord. A war is raging in the countryside around your home
in southern Ontario. Will you save your country, or will you be
cowed into submission?

1. You are eating dinner when you overhear American soldiers —
    the enemy — who are quartered in your house, talking. You . . .
    a. decide to listen more closely. > Go to question 2.
    b. ignore them. It's none of your business. > Go to question 3.
2. You overhear something that sounds dangerous. The Americans
    are plotting an attack! You . . .
    a. panic and do nothing. > Go to question 3.
    b. decide to take action. > Go to question 5.
3. You decide to start making a plum pudding. As you cook, your
    conscience gets the better of you. You . . .
    a. decide to let the British general know about the Americans'
    plans. > Go to question 4.
    b. write a secret message in code and hide it
    in the plum pudding. > Go to question 5.
4. You need to get through the American lines to
    the British general. You realize you will have
    to . . .
    a. sneak through in the dead of night, when
    no one will see you. > Go to question 6.
    b. disguise yourself in some way so no one
    realizes you are a spy for the British. > Go to
    question 7.
5. You finish cooking the pudding and . . .
    a. hide the code. > Go to question 10.
    b. it smells so good you wind up eating it. >
    Go to question 11.

6. You wait until dark. You put on a black dress and a black hat, and cover your face with your shawl. Then you . . .
   a. sneak out through your bedroom window. > Go to question 12.
   b. head for the front door. > Go to question 8.

7. You opt to disguise yourself as . . .
   a. a mime. No one suspects a thing. > MISSION ACCOMPLISHED.
   b. an American soldier. > Go to question 13.
   c. a typical Canadian girl, trying to drive her wandering cow home. > Go to question 9.

8. Whoops! You forgot that American soldiers are quartered in your house. They are sleeping in your front parlour, and you wake them when you open the door. One shouts, "Who's there?" You . . .
   a. say, "It's me, Laura." > Go to question 16.
   b. make a meowing sound. > Go to question 17.

9. You and your cow, Matilda . . .
   a. walk 30 km, through enemy lines. > Go to question 14.
   b. walk and walk and walk. > Go to question 15.

10. You tell the American officer stationed in your home that you need to deliver the plum pudding to your great aunt Sybil for her birthday. He agrees to take you. You . . .
    a. deliver the pudding to your great aunt, who is the general's sister. > Go to question 18.
    b. deliver the pudding to your great aunt, who is the general's wife. > Go to question 19.

11. Now that you are no longer hungry and can think straight, you decide you really need to let the British general know what's going on. You have no horse, but you put a saddle on your cow, Matilda, and ride over hill and dale to the British headquarters. You . . .

    a. tell the general your story. > He believes you! MISSION ACCOMPLISHED.

    b. try to catch your breath, but wind up having a coughing fit. > Go to question 20.

12. You jump out the window and sprain your ankle. > MISSION FAIL.

13. Unfortunately, you are too small to fit into the uniform you stole off a clothesline. The too-long legs drag on the ground and you trip, falling flat on your face in front of the American general. Oops. > MISSION FAIL.

14. No one stops you along the way. No one even notices you. You make it to British headquarters and deliver your message. > MISSION ACCOMPLISHED.

15. But Matilda really does like to wander. Eventually, she wanders in the wrong direction and you wind up in Muddy York. By the time you get Matilda turned around, the war is over. > MISSION FAIL.

16. They take one look at you in your black clothing and know you are up to no good. They march you back inside and question you. You tell them nothing, but you are unable to deliver your important message to the British general. > MISSION FAIL.

17. One soldier says, "That dumb cat," and goes back to sleep. The others start snoring too. You slip out into the night, evade enemy pickets and make it to British headquarters before daybreak. Message delivered. > MISSION ACCOMPLISHED.

18. The general's sister finds the message that evening when she eats the pudding, delivers it to her brother and saves the nation. > MISSION ACCOMPLISHED.

19. The general eats the pudding for dessert that evening, but because he does not see very well, he accidentally eats the message. > MISSION FAIL.

20. By the time you get to tell the general your story, he is so annoyed with you for ruining his dinner! And he doesn't believe you; you're just a crazy coughing kid, riding a cow! > MISSION FAIL , but you are so annoyed at him you decide to go off and join the Americans. You eventually become president.